# Dear Life
Maya C Popa

smith|doorstop

# the poetry business

Published 2022 by
Smith|Doorstop Books
The Poetry Business
Campo House,
54 Campo Lane,
Sheffield S1 2EG

Copyright © Maya C Popa 2022
All Rights Reserved

ISBN 978-1-914914-08-9
eBook ISBN 978-1-914914-09-6
Typeset by The Poetry Business
Printed by People for Print, Sheffield

Smith|Doorstop Books are a member of Inpress:
www.inpressbooks.co.uk

Distributed by NBN International, 1 Deltic Avenue,
Rooksley, Milton Keynes MK13 8LD

The Poetry Business gratefully acknowledges
the support of Arts Council England.

# Contents

| | |
|---|---|
| 5  | *Wound* is the Origin of Wonder |
| 7  | Margravine |
| 8  | Prayer |
| 10 | In the Museum of Childhood |
| 12 | On the Subject of Butterflies |
| 13 | Ghost Crabs |
| 14 | Reading |
| 15 | Genii Loci |
| 16 | Disquiet: A Taxonomy |
| 17 | Fife |
| 18 | Galileo Hosts Milton in Florence |
| 19 | The Peacocks |
| 20 | In Eden |
| 21 | The Owl |
| 23 | After |
| 24 | The Bends |
| 25 | Les Neiges D'Antan |
| 27 | How Far Can You See? |
| 28 | Dear Life |

# Wound *is the Origin of Wonder*

*Fiction is the house of many windows,*
    James said, and I sat at each one
        peering at a world

that trembled—or was that me instead,
    quivering in the face
        of all I made by looking,

unable to amend the plot or bend
    the hand? Like all falls, we came at ours
        by pleasure, all languages

seconded, learned by constraint—
    no way to say *look* and *away*
        and mean *un-lone me*.

Like gods, we made our kingdom hungry.
    Our appetites' agreement
        we called love,

though it was nearer the mirror
    than mercy. Sweet solstice,
        soul cousin, *Vita Nuova's*

Beatrice—do you hear our onceness
    beating at the door? How the past
        outlasts on either end,

though we'd like to burn out in oracular
    blindness. What doom
        to be beheld: you sing

when you should tremble. Will you leave me
    my wondering; will it be as when
        snow falls heavy on trees

and thou art felled?

# *Margravine*

> *We talked with each other about each other*
> *Though neither of us spoke – Emily Dickinson*

In the cemetery, the only available light
is shed by those wandering through,
tired, hungry, and a little put-off
to be stepping on the mouths of so many
once-people. We overlook the names
ambling towards one end which is a river,
which is always, somehow, a river.
I joke you brought me here to show me
your plot or to slay me in summer's
unabridged grass, though the joke's
that your hands will never be on me.
No future between us; we might as well be dead,
quoting Hardy to explain the little path
you sometimes take—like in a film you switch off
because life's short. Come midnight,
youths commit all sorts of crimes to prove
they're not afraid of what's coming for them.
They have the right idea, the wrong one,
or none. Either way, the grave. The flowers
growing furiously in their June bodies.
I lie about cemeteries all the time.
It's most alive at the heart of the thing
where the brush of your fingertips
against my wrist could send me begging.
*Hurry*, while we aren't dried up rivers.
While your mouth's not underfoot
in a permanent scream. It's most alive
at the heart of the thing, the only light,
a bright sheen given off by everything.

## *Prayer*

What runs through me could hardly be called piety.
It's not patience either, at least not by that name.
The pasture's dissolution into darkness,
the cow gnawing obediently without notion of infinity,
and stars—God, you know all about them.

Those evenings I was sure I'd die,
you were teaching me to live; I see that now.
And the gravity of all you did not say
but left me like a map for the intuiting.
Slowly, I saw the world for what it was,

or was it I who grew familiar, that long
habit of me? These were the pains
I was granted in this life: my face in cold weather,
a throbbing at the temples. And because
these occasionally left me, all secondary anguish,

I modeled after Yours. I swam in perpetual
end of spring knowing no summer could come of it,
used the same shears to trim a leaf of poison
and its remedy; I knew enough to know what I was doing.
So often I thought that I was clever, God,

and could see the spirit moving within me
like a school of fish darting under ice.
In the lit-up scan of my left breast,
bright dashes of calcium the beautiful doctor
used her needle to guide out of me.

A metal marker forever near my heart, my mother's heart,
her mother's—we are alive, and now, and still.
I'll tell you something I've never told a god:
all my life, I've been ready for a fight, been ready
for suffering. All my allowances came and spent

and all the coffers magically replenished.
Why galaxies, God? The fit of one palm
inside another? This ache of once—*I know, I know.*
Not piety: let me earn what I've got already.
My only prayer, *let this be enough.*

## In the Museum of Childhood

It's yours I remember,
and Larkin's, who called his
*a forgotten boredom.*

How it might just as well
have never happened,
though it did once,

it happened once, to you,
in a house with a moat
and no heating,

twin voices boiling over
in the kitchen below.
You'd survive it all,

which is to say, forsake;
those days turning in you
like a pinwheel still,

that base from which
all language understands
its failure. There was time

to be apart and still a part
of something human
before the usual forfeiture

of green to cities, days blunted
by the millstone of duty.
Now the hours blink back

with the eyes of roadside
animals, and the disks shrink
with not enough of anything

worth keeping. You could weep
for all you did not know then
was a blessing, the voices

hurt and angry but living
nonetheless, the highway throbbing
with its dreamed-of passages.

The museum makes converts
out of visitors—I lug youth's
icons inside me and believe:

we bear that loss we caused
by our arriving. We were never
loved by anything

the way tomorrow loved us then.

## On the Subject of Butterflies

Trying to write about them is hopeless,
those machinations colluding with air
Turgenev likened to withered maple.

Sentimental, resigned to knowing better,
and wondering still at the paperwork
of flight, armed with nets to breed

a tortured familiarity. Do they recognize
the desperation of our doing,
believing desire should end in evidence,

or after a life at ease with transformation,
are they so sure to be returned
to that first moment when anything

might still become of them
in fate's commanding and indifferent hand?

## *Ghost Crabs*

are mostly speculations on shape,
a way to say *ghost* with scientific
aplomb. They haunt a stretch
of Atlantic from Nantucket to Brazil,
their numbers dwindling like everything
that isn't us.

                Jeeps driving
down the beach pack the sand too firmly,
entombing the crabs in their burrows
overnight. I don't know that the world
was ever more forgiving, the lorries
less heavy with stolen bodies,
the drownings fewer over holiday weekends.

The ghost crabs come like spies
and it is beautiful to hope for them,
over the bright channels of the sea
and our unbright moorings.

                You will know
when it is time to mourn, they seem to say.
Today, I glimpse their rushed transparencies
and think, it could never be too early.

## *Reading*

The medium says it is a past-life connection;
*two* lives, she amends, at least two.

This, my life to mourn you,
to work through that other life

in which you died, a soldier, writing letters
from a border, and I never found a way

back into daylight. Needless to say,
this was not the good news I had hoped for.

I thought she'd offer something
conventionally hopeful, direct me

to a trapdoor I failed to see.
There was victory in the form

of wands or swords, I couldn't say which.
An end to grief so utter, I'm the mouth

it speaks with. What do I do?
Thread the past through the present's eye?

Ask that we meet in the blasted heath between?
She said, no, no, that won't be necessary.

Just forgive him: first for living, then for dying.
What are days for if not to let go of days.

## *Genii Loci*

All along, the world had referred to a real place
where it was hard to leave the car if parked too near a hedge.

To race the body towards pleasure in the backseat
held no appeal, though the image had its salvageable moments,
the hand that gripped the wheel gentling the flesh,
hitch of breath at an unexpected angle.

*Not for us*, we said, chastened by memory's make-believe.

Besides, the humiliating inelegance,
the onlookers with rucksacks that double as sleeping bags,
the ones with binoculars come expressly for the doggers,
watching couples strip down to what's left at the beginning.

No appetite so large it could not be filled
behind closed doors, we agreed, a joke we'd return to politely.

About the animal of the body, I have learned
it's in no hurry to be sated or stilled.
It lives to serve the error that confounds it,
to argue over buttons in the mind's backseat.

No imagination safe enough from love
which swears by a map that leads nowhere.

We could drive ourselves and each other out with it,
could wave goodbye or wait; we could never stop waiting.

# *Disquiet: A Taxonomy*

I want to love someone I worry
is me, though it's just as often you
I worry I love when I mistake
the spoken for the intuited,
the ice for the fish beneath.

How the Buddhist described
desire's oculus, how the artist
picked a flower from a vase
and used it to paint flowers
fills me with worry. The difference

between irony and allegory,
telling mountain from molehill
or landmine. I worry I'll only
have words with which
to tell the story of what mostly

occurred outside language,
like a doctor treating for
the wrong ailment, which
doctors often do, much to
my worry. See, it's like a sun

where your voice lives in memory,
like moonlight on water—
the mixed simile worries.
*Most people are dreaming
of someone else, it's what keeps
the jukebox playing all night.*

I'm worried Willie Nelson was right.

## *Fife*

The white sun has her way here,
raising a fog like an atomized star
over ruins
and the heron standing on one leg.

Listen: everything is listening
to the North Sea retreating
like a voice before sleep.

Out there, the beloved
is slipping through time; otherwise,
you might see without inquiry.

When will the fog lift,
by what doing?

A faint hiss like a stone's lament.

A faint hiss—that is
your own life now, hurrying
from one light into another.

## *Galileo Hosts Milton in Florence*

Hard to say if what they saw
was geometry or God,
galaxies roiling wordlessly
each night, a summary of light
painted fresh across the firmament.

Ink bringing daybreak into Eden,
the angels, listless in their graces,
latent good pooling with nothing
to war over. For all that was fair
was sure to fall those days,

the voice of novelty whispered
from the lamb's wool.
A jug of water on the table
between them, like an artifact
of loneliness, the telescope's

moons on Satan's shield—
it was, after all, a human
friendship, full of mortality's
tokens. Both men
went blind in their old age.

Begin again in darkness,
life says sometimes.
Imagine the trees burning
in autumn, the earth's
relief, at last, at being fallen.

## *The Peacocks*

in Holland Park don't care who loves them.
They're like stones at the bottom of rivers
and it's only our wandering that brings them
into focus, its own kind of foreboding.
I could walk here in the dark with you,
silent as the feather caught in the eaves.
It's not only color and scale that endears them.
It's the way they can't be conceived of fully
without blinking back a dread at splendor
so near a public waste bin, the likelihood of failure.
The staccato of orange against blue—really,
how much more will this world enrage us
with its beauty, even as it leans towards last
assessments. And haven't I minded you like this,
a cartographer patiently charting planets?
Haven't I taken that footpath down
a woodland labeled *dark; do not enter; idle; want*.
Oh, but for the ode of it. The life that can't
be lived behind the eyelids. And you,
a fruit there somewhere in the branches.
A bird that will not scare or fly.

## *In Eden*

There were reasons not to eat.
For one, a snake that spoke in meter,
and the light falling just so
on the fruit of Baroque still-life.

On earth, it's sleep that interrupts
the feeding. Still, your hands
will find me in a dream,
and I'll bring them to my lips

though they're nothing like the quince.
I'd like to be less hungry,
placid like a saint, with nothing
but polite appreciation for the world.

Maybe then I'd find the living
reasonable to part with,
the blue moons and the red ones
seasonally beheld—and people—

their expressions like indentations
on water. I'd row out to that
horizon where nothing needs,
at last at ease with the order of things.

In Eden, everything answered
when you called it, the snake
already knowing all our names.

## *The Owl*

Took off from the field again
    away from you and back in my direction.

We share an owl now—we did not mean
    for this to happen. It hovers

between us, a symbol and debt, sleeps
    in a country neither recognizes

until we're face to face—then, it's familiar,
    and it's impossible not to laugh.

*Of course, there's an owl.* You're the owl
    in the belfry set off by noon bells.

I'm the owl circling the wounded land.
    Among the difficulties of caring

for something metaphorical
    is the guarantee it will one day

become something else, and it's hard to say
    for certain when the transformation's final.

How you woke one morning at a job
    you hated, in a mind you'd wrestled

into gentleness, and nothing made sense
    except the way I listened.

You burned for me; the owl was a candle
    by whose flame I could see

my own value clearly: the second chance,
    the double life tiptoed warily around.

The feeling only a wild bird knows
    whose head turns 270 degrees,

is silent in flight and blends
    with its settings, whose talons can

withstand any sort of landing. That,
    a neckless wonder, strips

ligament from flesh. Something so polite
    about enduring its violence

and hoping only to remain in favor,
    watch the bones assemble

in the shape of a vole. There are ways
    to fail an owl, for metaphor to fail.

I remember you—the dusk
    we wrought by listening.

The long hunt we made of night.

## *After*

Skymiles of starlings over the penitentiary.

December a descant and a North Star
like a North Star.

Twice a day, the sun.

The hand of wind over the mountains.

The rest will become, disappear by becoming.

Dark of plenty, of fracture. God's dark
of perfect recall.

What earth is this if not ripe for threshing?

*What joy it was, and how we knew what joy it was.*

## The Bends

When the doctor sliced open the body,
soft still to the touch, apprenticed
to expression, when the flesh

was pulled back between index and thumb
revealing the armour of breastbone,
imagine he who saw the heart froth,

the heart bubble over like soda water.
Then think of grief leaving the body,
flitting like salt to the nearby sink,

and joy like atoms joining in air
towards another living promise.
Under the night of millions of gallons

of water, the man had been building
the Brooklyn Bridge, rinsing off
the day's labors in streams warm

and patient, rain-like now. *The bends*
after the posture assumed by the afflicted
as nitrogen crept up the spine's steps.

There are still things that cannot be imagined.
The indifferent light on the surface of
the water. The wounding breath of air.

## *Les Neiges D'Antan*

In Lyon, the lovers of the past
are picking up handfuls
of powdered snow.

I watch them in the video
a friend sends colored
in confectionary pastels.

They are safe from the fear
of the world boiling over,
sons lost along the German border.

Villon asked about the snows
of yesteryear sensing there'd been
a diminishment perhaps.

It wasn't that long ago
we walked in autumn,
the silence between us

its own snow, our longing
the language of manuscripts
illuminated painstakingly by hand.

I didn't bend. You didn't.
We were wintered by the thought.
But the lovers are rushing

towards where the clip fades
into immovable darkness.
It will be 1914, the fatal cough,

the Hiroshima Mosler safe.
It will be a trying age
and then another.

It's plain we didn't see
the future coming. Even spring
came and left as a surprise.

Where are you now, snow
that vanishes with touch,
snow which cannot be

sped up but sleeps
where the past falls,
is always falling.

## *How Far Can You See?*

A mile, a meter, twenty?

Billions of miles
into the pyres of past stars—

or farther, past the hills
through the window
of the woman you first loved
who played the harp?

It's a start. *How* do you see?

The children, you said,
choose obvious distances,

not the moon made local
on the surface of the water,
not the train's doppler
in the salt mines of the ear.

What I mean, a sort
of speechlessness,
though the words insist
on livable houses.

*Shut your eyes*, they say—
*there is nothing here to see.*

## *Dear Life*

I can't undo all I have done to myself,
what I have let an appetite for love do to me.

I have wanted all the world, its beauties
and its injuries; some days,
I think that is punishment enough.

Often, I received more than I'd asked,

which is how this works—you fish in open water
ready to be wounded on what you reel in.

Throwing it back was a nightmare.
Throwing it back and seeing my own face

as it disappeared into the dark water.

Catching my tongue suddenly on metal,
spitting the hook into my open palm.

Dear life: I feel that hook today most keenly.

Would you loosen the line—you'll listen

if I ask you,

if you are the sort of life I think you are.

# *Acknowledgements*

My gratitude to *The Atlanic, American Poetry Review, Inque, Jewish Currents, PN Review, Poetry London, Poetry, The London Magazine, Poetry Ireland, The New Statesman, The TLS, Wildness Journal,* and *The Bridport Prize Anthology,* in which some of these poems first appeared.